Pennsylvania Avenue

Report of the President's Temporary Commission on Pennsylvania Avenue

Every President and every Congress, through L'Enfant's inspiration, has had some part in the planning of this Avenue and Mall. We have now come full circle—to the simple but grand design of two centuries ago. It is my hope that the present plan will provide an island of refuge, great in scale, strong in axial relationships, and safe from the motorcar, where one may experience a sense of joie de vivre and renewed pride in this National Capital.

— Nathaniel Alexander Owings,
Chairman

from *The Grand Design,* 1967

Contents

Foreword

Anyone involved with the development of the nation's capital can be thought in a legitimate sense to have the American people for a client. The people of the District of Columbia have additional special claims on the attention of the planner. So also the Congress. But for all the general truth of such assertions, the preeminent fact is that the patron of the Federal City is the President of the United States. A half century cycle of sorts seems to be at work. There have been four periods of intensive development, and in each the presidential influence has been uppermost. First with Washington and Jefferson in the period of L'Enfant; next with Grant in the era of "Boss" Shepherd; then Theodore Roosevelt and the McMillan Commission in the early years of the century; finally John F. Kennedy, followed by Lyndon B. Johnson and now President Nixon, in the 1960's.

As is widely known, the current period of concern for the design of the city began with President Kennedy in the course of the very few thoroughly relaxed moments permitted an American president: on the ride back from the Capitol to the White House on Inauguration Day! The great ceremonies of the Republic completed; the anguish of power about to begin. Looking to the north side of Pennsylvania Avenue, the "via sacra" of this quadrennial ritual, the signs were unmistakable. Life was rapidly going out of the heart of the city. Parcels of land were being collected. Soon office buildings would rise in unbroken series. The Capitol would be cut off from the living city as surely as the Sub-treasury on Wall Street is cut off from the life of Manhattan. On the south side, the Federal Triangle stood with dignity, and with what increasingly could be appreciated as architectural design of a very high quality indeed. But unfinished. The depression of the 1930's had come, and with it the great circle of 12th Street had stopped in mid arc; the north portion of the Grand Plaza, from 12th to 14th Streets had ceased construction, while the plaza itself remained

1

a parking lot. Kennedy remarked on the situation to his Secretary of Labor, Arthur Goldberg, and just as promptly forgot the matter. But there was energy to spare in those days, and by late summer the undertaking had begun. A council was formed, offices were borrowed. At length a plan began to take shape, emerging from the logic and necessities of what had gone before.

Word began to reach Kennedy in the White House. His sure sense of the historic told him that this now mattered. Almost the last direction he gave before leaving for Dallas was that on his return he wished the Pennsylvania Avenue model placed in the Fish Room of the West Wing of the White House and a coffee hour set, on which occasion he could expound the plan and explain its importance to the nation. Horsky, Walton and I were sitting down to lunch to arrange just that when the White House switch board rang.

＊　＊　＊

In these years the nation has come increasingly to view the routine and endlessly reported state of urban decline and social decay of the inner city in terms of "crisis." And the perception is not far wrong. What is misleading is the presumed corollary of some dramatic and finite response that will put an end to such crises. This will not happen, and the expectation that it might will only deepen the torment of the moment. What is open to us is the patient, even at times plodding, effort by men of large purpose to take, one by one, the small steps that lead somewhere. This has been the lot of those who have worked through the 1960's with the intent that here in the Nation's Capital along Pennsylvania Avenue we might build the first fully modern, fully human inner city setting in the nation, possibly in the world. It will also be the lot of those who carry on the effort in the 1970's. It has been reward enough to see the issue nudged ever so slightly upwards on the agendas of the presidency and the citizenry alike.

—Daniel P. Moynihan
Vice Chairman

Introduction

Five years after its redevelopment was first proposed, Pennsylvania Avenue is today in the grip of change. Vast construction operations are visible at the foot of Capitol Hill, along the route of the North Central expressway, at the site of the FBI building. A foretaste of the future is provided at 12th Street by the new Presidential Building, with its arcade, 50-foot setback, special paving and landscaping to illustrate what is planned for the Avenue as a whole. Far more changes are ahead, authorized in Congressional enactments, executive decisions, and the plans of private builders of office buildings, hotels and other projects. Truly, here is a plan well launched towards completion.

Irreversible as it may be, the Pennsylvania Avenue plan is still susceptible to important changes. Its rate of progress as well as its development in detail will be influenced by many decisions still to be taken. Yet within this well-established framework of work under way, it is not the details but the conception of Pennsylvania

Model of the proposed Pennsylvania Avenue looking from the Capitol to the White House.

3

Avenue as a whole—the grand route connecting the Capitol and the President's House—that inspires the future.

That great vision, provided in the recommendations of the President's Advisory Council on Pennsylvania Avenue in 1964, is securely rooted in the past. From the beginning of the city in 1789 the goal of a unified monumental city, "a capital city worthy of the nation" in the phrase most often heard in Congress, has been pursued. In decisions about parks and buildings, about the relation of the city to its surrounding hills and rivers, about the centralization or decentralization of the administrative establishment, about appropriations and appointments—this goal has been the beacon towards which national efforts were steadfastly directed.

The designation in 1965 of Pennsylvania Avenue as a National Historic Site, linking in reciprocity of sight the legislative and executive centers of the nation, confirmed inevitably almost two centuries of labor. What better signal of the national Bicentennial in 1976 than the completion of this project, whose location, civic spaces and new buildings invite so many appropriate activities of commemoration and celebration? Here is the nation's pulse, its present as well as its past. Here are its legislators and executive leaders as well as its historic landmarks, monuments and documents. And here is an example of civic art for cities the world over, intent upon their self-improvement and re-establishment as a focus of human values.

Important Federal projects punctuate the Pennsylvania Avenue development, but the plan itself advances the city as a whole. It provides once again what the Avenue has been in the city's history, splendid living room where all of its citizens can congregate, not simply for occasions of ceremony but for the daily urban pleasures of business and work in agreeable settings, shopping and dining in attractive and stimulating surroundings, and relaxation in promenades and gardens. The plan strengthens the broader efforts to reinvigorate the commercial heart of Washington as the center of a metropolis. It exploits the new mass transit system and contributes to its success. It reaches north to strengthen efforts to rebuild the riot-torn areas and south to serve increasing millions of visitors to the city.

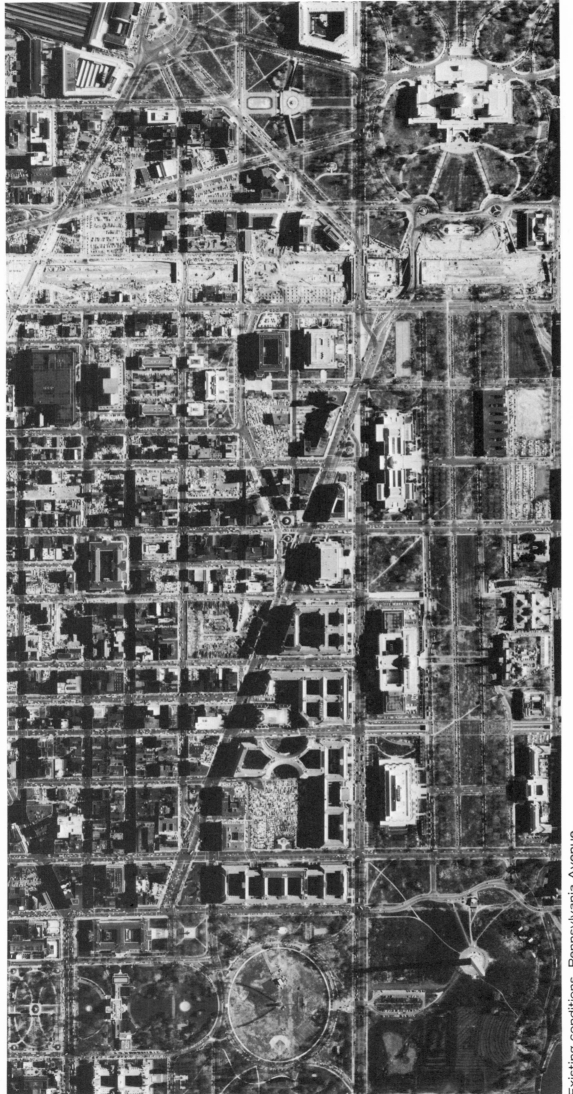

Existing conditions, Pennsylvania Avenue.

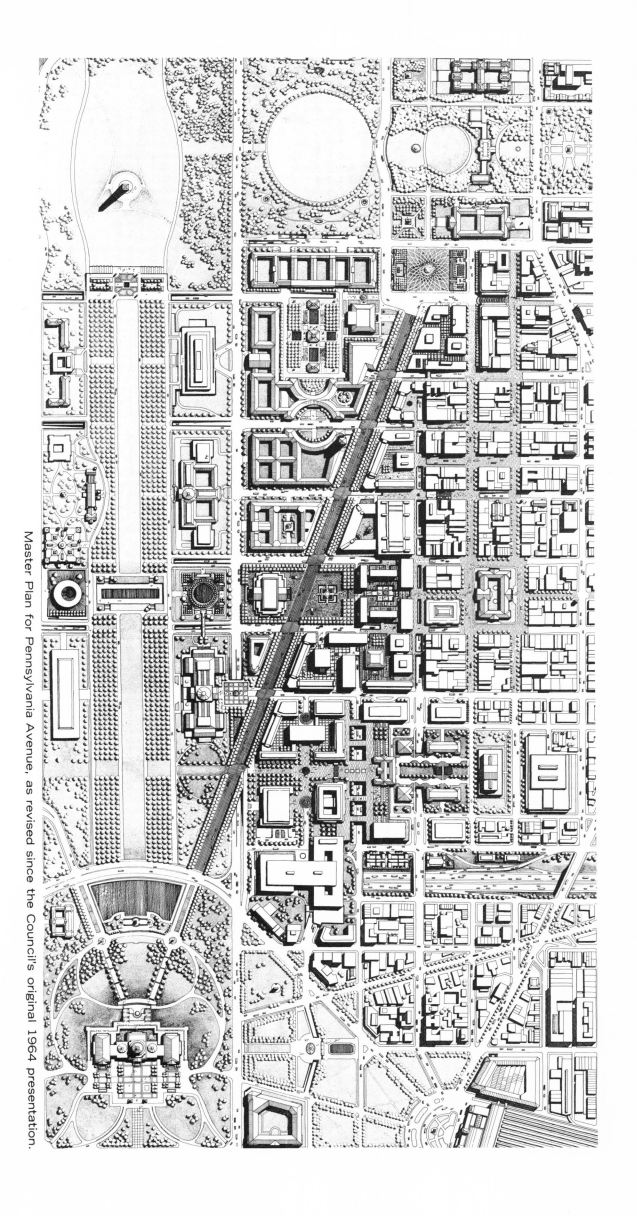

Master Plan for Pennsylvania Avenue, as revised since the Council's original 1964 presentation.

The spirit of the plan is contemporary. It seizes and employs the very forces of technology, growth and change that have threatened the destruction of so many large cities. The threat of impersonal bigness has been curbed by more humanly scaled designs. Streams of traffic that have destroyed the street and the sidewalk have been redirected and regulated both to speed their movement and to protect the pedestrian's world. Developments that threaten to pollute the urban environment with noise and fumes have been redesigned and relocated to conform to standards of basic human decency. The result is a city—certainly a very important part of a large and significant city—that will be fit for living and enjoyment.

Even to the millions who know Washington on television, the visual quality of the city will be enormously enhanced. Nearly half a century after the building of the impressively unified facades of the Federal Triangle, a more varied but equally unified north side of Pennsylvania Avenue will look south into the sunlight of a new day. Ornamental paving, special street furniture and lighting, street graphics, fountains and sculpture, arcaded buildings of uniform setback and height but for varying purposes announced in their architectures— these will create a richly designed special street whose excitement will be communicated as a strong image even to those who may never see it in reality.

In the great tradition of city planning that Washington has always expressed, the rebuilding of Pennsylvania Avenue should find a place in the nation's heart as a fitting tribute to its national aspiration. It is an achievement to fill the nation with pride. The architect selected by President Washington was a great dreamer. But L'Enfant, like so many of the City's later planners, was not a great achiever. The opportunity of today, presented by the plan steadily developed further by the Pennsylvania Avenue Commission, is to realize a great conception which embraces so much of what the city and the national government desire, and to do so with a dispatch which rivals the imagination and style of the plan itself.

Capitol Reflecting Pool

From the west terrace of the Capitol, rising 80 feet above the Potomac valley, the basic Triangle of Pierre Charles L'Enfant's grand geometry can be fully seen, a design unmatched in grandeur by any city in the world. L'Enfant set the Capitol in a star of avenues like those invented for the hunting forests of royalty and formalized at Versailles, but which heralded the end of absolutism by creating no single dominating center. The Capitol, the White House and the Washington Monument today stand at the points of this triangle as if to symbolize the distributed power of the new democracy. Lavish corridors of open space, Pennsylvania Avenue and the Great Mall, are the mile-long arms of the Triangle, stretching from the Capitol to the White House on the north, and to the white obelisk of the Monument on the south. The unity of the nation is here made visible by the unity of space achieved over a vast area.

The President's Temporary Commission on Pennsylvania Avenue has sought to realize the full intent of the founders of the Republic, so marvelously reflected in the bold design of the capitol's first planner. Thus the Commission's main objective has been to restore the

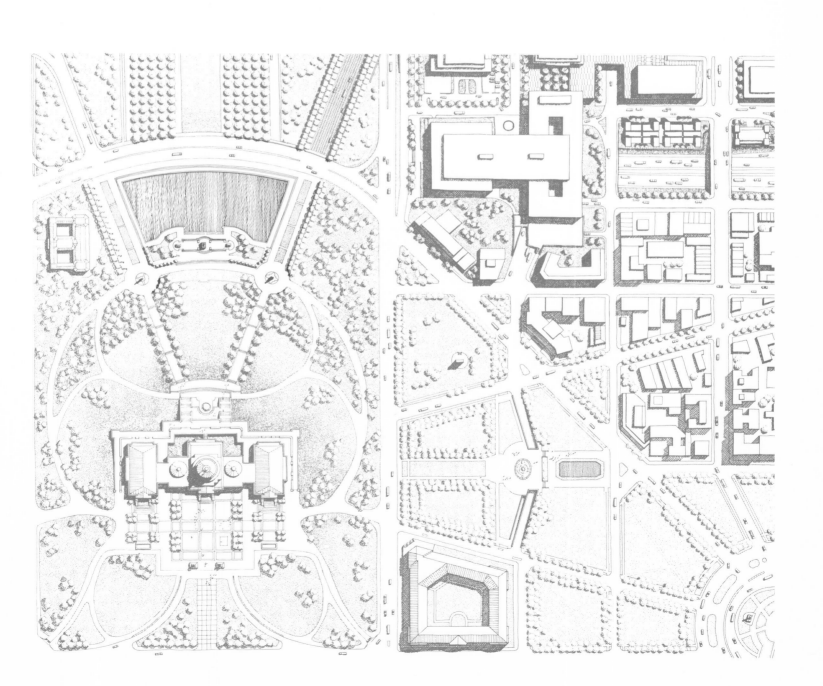

Avenue and the Mall for use by the people. Design decisions towards this end follow a basic plan for controlling the automobile traffic that has degraded the capital for either efficient or pleasurable use by its people. Both through and local traffic are routed underground in strategic sectors between the Capitol and the White House. A great freeway is thus brought to the very foot of the Capitol without encroaching on this historic site. The surface area preserved will accommodate a five-acre reflecting pool and pedestrian plaza now under construction.

After most streets now crossing the Mall are closed to surface traffic and local east-west traffic is carried through an underground tunnel and depressed roadway along the present path of E Street, the visitor standing on the west terrace may look out on the entire panorama of L'Enfant's composition in space and, perhaps for the first time, be able to sense its meaning for the human values to which this government was dedicated.

The Capitol Reflecting Pool, presently under construction.

Proposed Capitol Reflecting Pool and Ceremonial Drive.

10

Construction work at the Pool site.

11

The freedom of pedestrian movement is immediately achieved in a plaza with a sparkling pool in which the solid mass of the huge Capitol dome will itself become fluid as it is reflected. This fitting symbol provides a foretaste of the splendors the larger plan offers the city and its people. Like other parts of the plan, the reflecting pool is made possible by modern technology. Engineering skills and industrial techniques make it possible to transform the highway's threat of destruction into a civic opportunity.

Inaugural parades—the first of which was Thomas Jefferson's second inaugural procession on horseback down Pennsylvania Avenue from the Capitol to the President's House—may in the future choose their routes from the simplified street pattern around Capitol Hill. Louisiana Avenue will extend across the Mall as a ceremonial drive in front of the Reflecting Pool, just east of the present path of 1st Street. With 1st, 2nd and 3rd Streets closed and planted with grass and trees, Louisiana Avenue will become an uninterrupted cross-link to Union Station Plaza. It will carry local traffic only; through traffic will use the tunnel freeway underneath the pool.

Plan for the Capitol Reflecting Pool and Ceremonial Drive.

Vertical section through the Center Leg Freeway under the Pool.

12

There are several possible routes for the Inaugural Parade as it leaves the Capitol. Forming as usual at the Capitol East Front, the parade could circle north on Northwest Drive to Pennsylvania Avenue. Or the Parade could move south on Southwest Drive and then north on Ceremonial Drive itself to Pennsylvania Avenue. As a third possibility, the Inaugural Parade could form quite simply on the West Capitol Front in the splendid setting created by the reflecting pool, then move directly down Pennsylvania Avenue. The Inaugural Parade has never conformed to a set diagram; its future choice of route will be related to the general revision of the Capitol Grounds now under consideration by the Architect of the Capitol.

Artist's sketch of the Capitol Reflecting Pool.

13

Labor Building

North of the Reflecting Pool and in full view of the Capitol, the new Labor Department building is rising on foundations spanning the Center Leg Freeway tunnel between 2nd and 3rd Streets. On the west, the building spans 3rd Street.

With the roar and fumes of traffic below ground, the Capitol's surroundings can be recaptured for new buildings and pedestrian use. The building also answers the request made in 1964 by the President's Advisory Council on Pennsylvania Avenue, predecessor of this Commission, for a "traffic barrier to lessen the noise and obscure the view of freeway traffic entering the Mall tunnel." At the north end of the building, northbound traffic will exit from the tunnel by a ramp up to truncated 2nd Street, and southbound traffic will enter the tunnel.

Construction of the Labor building and the freeway tunnel beneath it, begun in July 1968 by the Federal Public Buildings Service and the District of Columbia Highway Department, reverses the usual air rights arrangement by which a state highway department, as owner of the land, leases the right to build above an interstate highway to a public or private developer. By

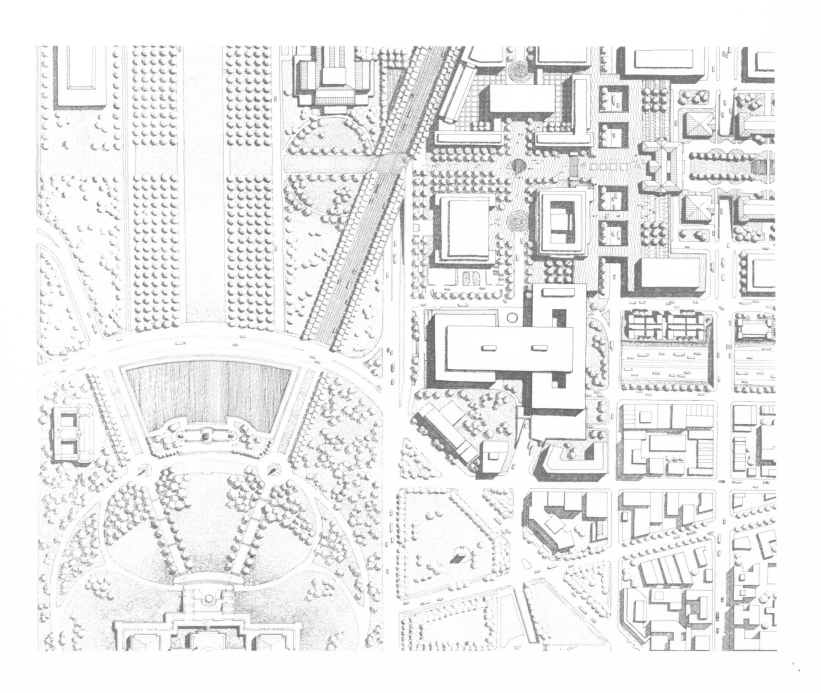

law, the Federal government must own the land on which its buildings are constructed. Therefore, in this case, the District government had to purchase the street and highway "easement" rights from the Federal builder-owner for half the cost of the Labor building site.

The Highway Department is also paying for the tunnel and its ventilation and ramps. The Federal government is paying for foundations, garages and basement areas of the building. This work will be completed in two years at a cost of $14 million. Construction of the rest of the building is scheduled to begin in 1970 and to be completed in three years.

The Labor building will house half the system to supply and exhaust air for the 15-lane highway tunnel (8 traffic lanes plus entry, exit, and pull-off lanes), described

Future site for the Labor Building, showing the Center Leg Freeway, under construction.

15

as the world's largest in traffic carried. The other half of the ventilating system will be installed in the proposed Health, Education and Welfare building planned for the south side of the Mall. Both installations will have two 60-foot-high exhaust stacks as shown in the section drawing of the Labor building (page 17) taken through the Constitution Avenue frontage; the two-level garage at the left of the tunnel is one of three underground parking areas providing for 600 cars.

Steel girders with a 70-foot span carry the building above the highway; the clear span houses service functions and forms a buffer zone against the noise and vibration of the highway. In the plaza areas, the mass of the soil used for landscaping also gives acoustic protection.

Proposed Labor Building over the Center Leg Freeway.

Despite its great size and the formidable technical problems faced by its designers, the Labor building promises to be an inviting structure that will do its part to rescue the heart of the city from the automobile. Embracing wholeheartedly the objectives of the Pennsylvania Avenue plan, the building's designers have worked to encourage pedestrian movement. Walkers may easily enter the building on three sides (the fourth is pre-empted by freeway ramps), and three underground garages provide ramp entry near building corners out of the way of the pedestrian path.

The huge building for 6000 workers is modulated to human scale. Deep landscaped plazas penetrate the building, bringing in light and air along with thousands of walkers, many of whom are expected to arrive by the new subway planned to stop at adjacent Judiciary Square. The outdoor plazas are linked inside the building by a hall 30 feet high, providing a walk-through from Judiciary Square and the Municipal Center on the west to the Capitol grounds on the east. Off the hall are meeting rooms for labor negotiators and an auditorium. The free use of glass in the building walls gives this material's unique message: whatever business is done here is open to public view.

Architect's rendering of the Labor Building looking from Municipal Center.

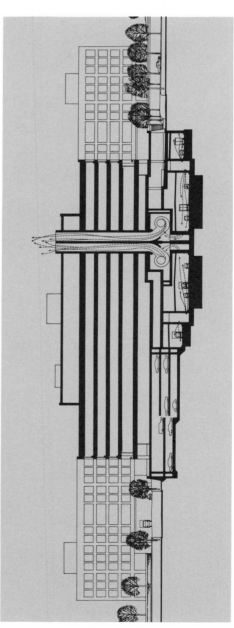

Vertical section through the Labor Building and the Center Leg Freeway, looking north.

National Gallery - Judiciary Square

The design of an addition to the National Gallery of Art at the juncture of the Avenue and the Mall crystallizes the endeavor of the Pennsylvania Avenue plan to achieve new urban grandeur. Contemporary architectural design is distinguished not by a given style, material, or technology, but by its characteristic concern to provide as intimately and deftly as possible for the many needs of all who use, visit, or merely look at buildings. No U.S. architect is more qualified than I. M. Pei to meet the stylistic problem posed by adding to the 800 tons of rose-white Tennessee marble in the Graeco-Roman forms designed by John Russell Pope in the 1930's. Pei emphasizes that the addition will be the "working part of the museum" and thus "completely different in purpose and appearance from the present building." However, he does plan at this time to use similar materials and to conform to the existing building setback lines.

In purpose, the National Gallery addition will exemplify the current trend of our best museums by be-

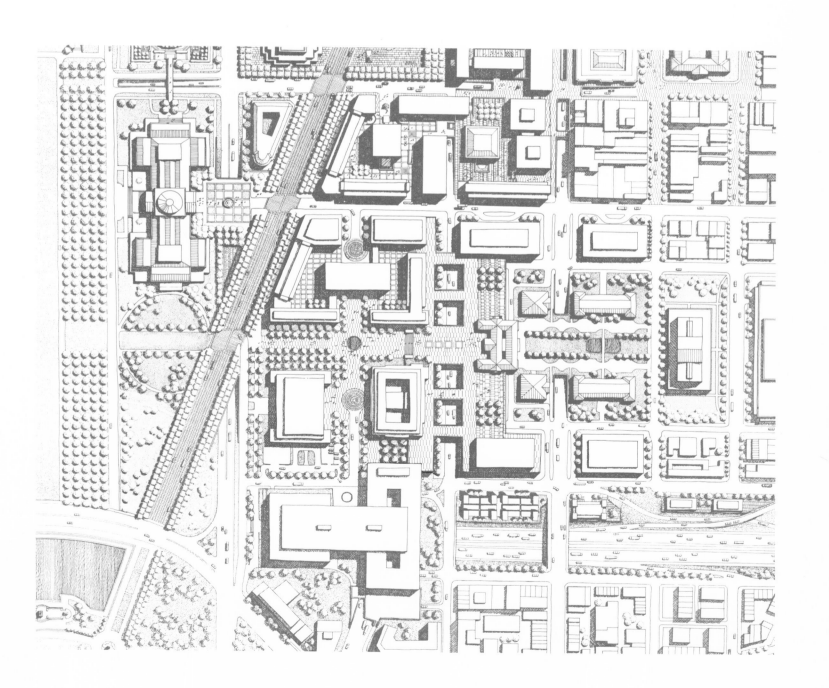

coming not a marble storehouse for the art of the past but a boisterous fountain of ideas for the arts of living in the present. It will house changing exhibits, a Center for Advanced Study in the Visual Arts, and working space for staff, especially the Gallery's Extension Service now reaching 3000 American communities. Pei and his associates are in the initial design and programming stages and have not yet revealed a definitive design for the new building.

The addition to the National Gallery will on its northern side face what is now the most congested intersection along Pennsylvania Avenue. Here Pennsylvania's great diagonal, moving southeast to the Capitol to form part of the constellation of avenues envisioned by L'Enfant, meets the intersection of Constitution Avenue and 4th Street in the grid pattern imposed by Washington and Jefferson. The result is a six-way traffic jam and eyesore.

Congested intersection of Pennsylvania Avenue, Constitution Avenue and 4th Street.

The National Gallery of Art and to the left the proposed site for the East Building.

19

Model of the National Gallery of Art and the completed Constitution Avenue Underpass.

The Pennsylvania Avenue planners have proposed carrying Constitution Avenue below Pennsylvania by means of an underpass and reserving 4th Street south of the Avenue for pedestrian access to the two gallery buildings and to the Mall. The present path of 4th Street north of the Avenue will also become a broad pedestrian walkway (renamed John Marshall Place) leading north to the long-hoped-for D.C. Municipal Center. The District Government has retained a local architectural firm to further refine the planning for the area. Their recommendations should be forthcoming in the near future.

In front of the National Gallery, 6th Street interrupts the Avenue with the now isolated Mellon Memorial Fountain. The Avenue planners propose to remove this awkward triangle and move the splendid fountain to a new forecourt to the National Gallery. Sixth Street would bridge Constitution Avenue and terminate in what might be most appropriately called Mellon Square in honor of the Gallery's donor, Andrew Mellon. Mellon's son and daughter, Paul Mellon and Mrs. Mellon Bruce, have given some $20 million for building and staffing the addition to the Gallery, due to open in 1973.

Artist's sketch of the National Gallery Plaza above the Constitution Avenue Underpass.

21

E Street Distributor

The roar of automobile and truck traffic has in large part prevented the pedestrian's response to the architectural environment. The experience of the university campus or the cathedral close is denied the walker in the city, who nowadays scarcely sees the buildings, obscured as they are by moving traffic, or regards them at his peril as he competes with high-speed machines for his place in the city. The span of the human eye is still a constant of architectural design, as it has been throughout history, but the opportunity to design for it has diminished in Washington as it has in Paris and Florence and other historic cities.

Today heavy cross-town traffic moves along the Avenue, threatening without discrimination the amenities of the passer-by and the residents of the White House themselves. But the greatest casualty is likely to be the city. Government has a special responsibility to return the capital to its proper use by the people. The plan creates new space both above and below the present streets, and assigns different levels to separate the various uses now competing for a single space: walking, driving, parking, shopping.

Artist's sketch of the Pedestrian Shelf above the E Street Distributor.

22

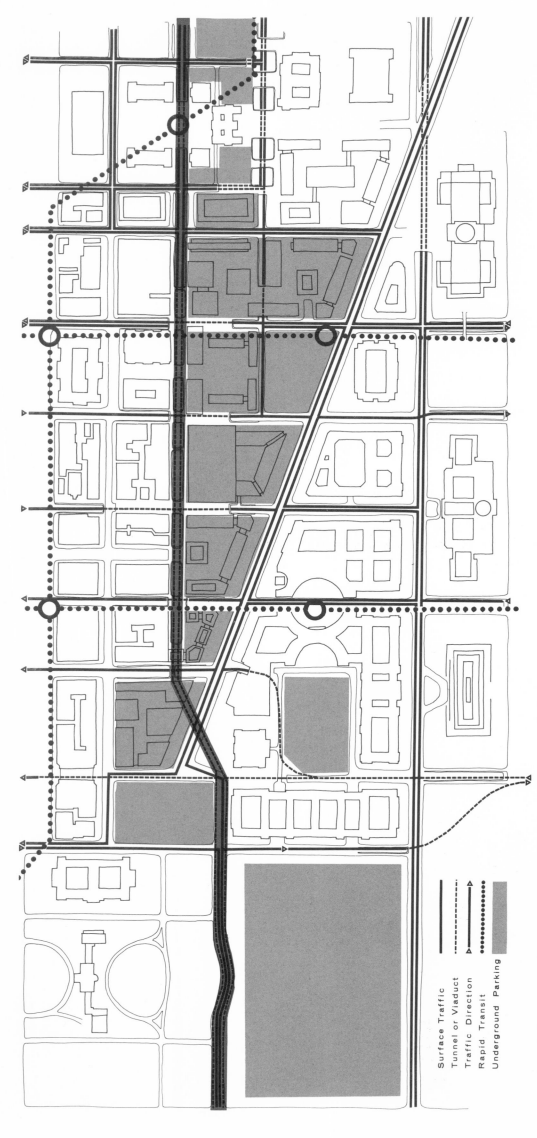

Proposed E Street traffic pattern and related underground parking.

Surface Traffic
Tunnel or Viaduct
Traffic Direction
Rapid Transit
Underground Parking

Basic in this plan is upgrading E Street, today a secondary east-west street moving across the core of downtown Washington, to accept the major traffic of the area. As a distributor, with links to the inner-loop freeway on the east and the E Street Expressway on the west, it will play a decisive role in traffic and parking management affecting the quality of the Avenue as a whole. By depressing E Street along a six-block segment of its present path, benefits will be realized by both the established business community to the north and the government center to the south. It will more strongly link these two parts of the city.

The street, widened to accommodate both traffic lanes and ramp lanes leading to underground parking, will dominate the lower level. Above is a shelf that will be sacred to the pedestrian. Located to take advantage of the natural land slope from F Street down to Pennsylvania Avenue, this broad shelf extends from F, Washington's main shopping street, over both the tunneled and depressed segments of the new E Street roadway. Buildings now located on this roadway will be able to maintain their present street access over a transition period. New buildings will be planned for pedestrian access from the shelf, while automobile and

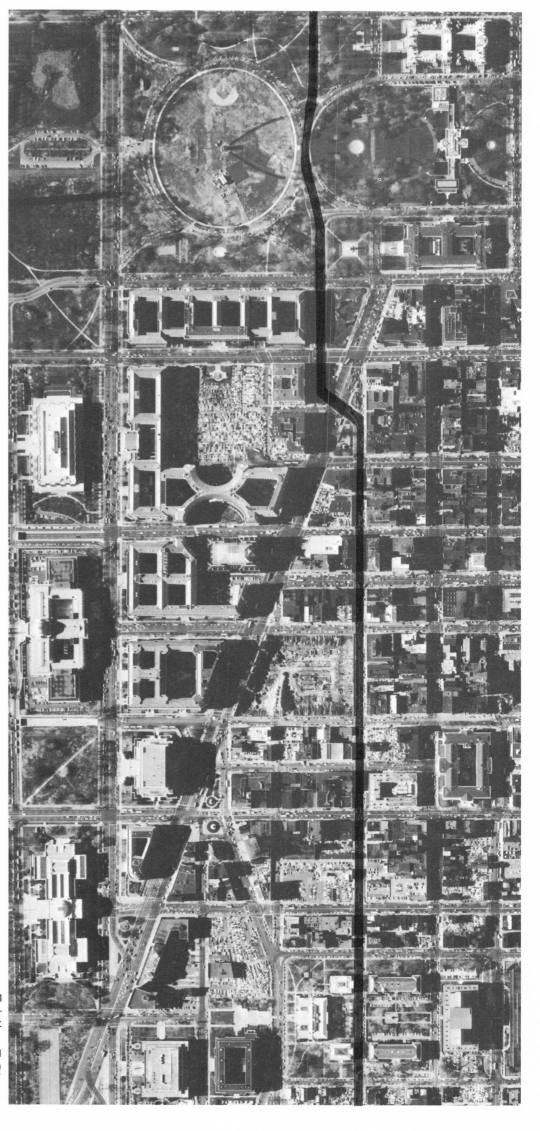

Existing E Street.

24

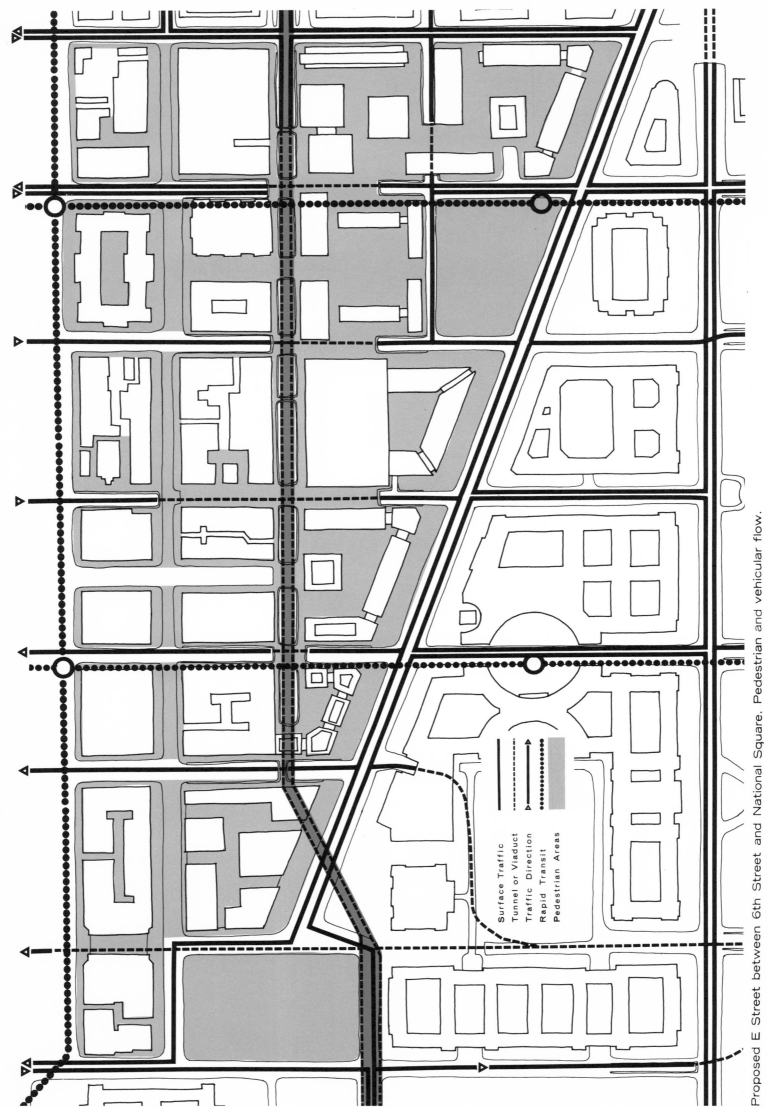

Surface Traffic
Tunnel or Viaduct
Traffic Direction
Rapid Transit
Pedestrian Areas

Proposed E Street between 6th Street and National Square. Pedestrian and vehicular flow.

25

truck traffic will enter at an underground level for both deliveries and parking.

One of Washington's most characteristic sights is the outpouring of government employees at the end of the day's work, and the exodus from the Federal Triangle is an outstanding spectacle of this sort. These rush-hour swarms, intent upon reaching their bus stop, car pool or other destination, will find the pedestrian shelf a major distributor for their busy foot traffic. But walkers will also use the shelf to move in a continuous path in all directions throughout the planning area, using stairs, ramps, and escalators to filter down to Pennsylvania Avenue and at least two levels of underground parking below. Openings in the shelf above E Street will give light and ventilation to the roadway below. Pedestrian levels will be enlivened by provision of small shops and other amenities.

As an example, a shopper on F Street could move out along the shelf over E Street, pass through an outdoor art show or a sculpture garden, stop at an outdoor tree-shaded restaurant and finally move down to Pennsylvania Avenue by stair or ramp and cross it to reach, say, the National Gallery. Or he might retrace part of his path and descend directly to the subway which will be running underground below 12th Street.

Traffic proceeding west on E Street will pass under National Square and serve the parking garages under that square and the Ellipse. Access to the Ellipse

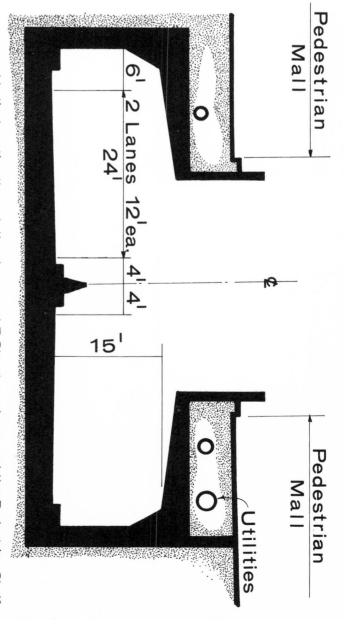

Vertical section through the depressed E Street roadway and the Pedestrian Shelf.

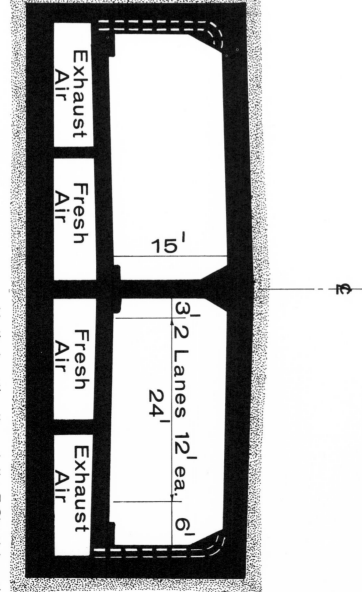

Vertical section through the E Street tunnel.

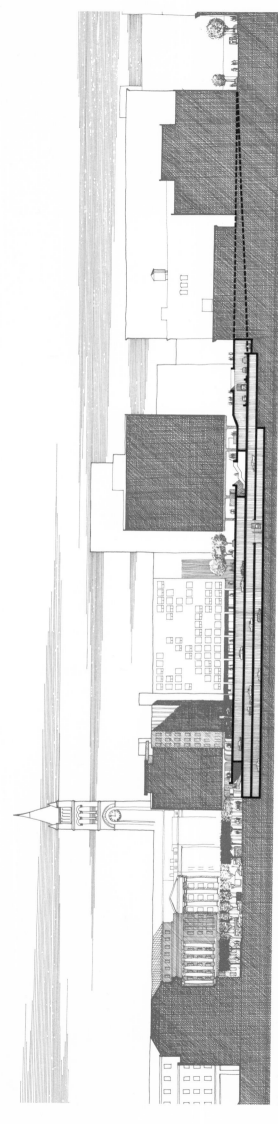

Vertical section, F Street to Pennsylvania Avenue. The Pedestrian Shelf, parking, F Street and depressed E Street levels are shown in black.

garage will also be possible from a continuation of the present E Street Expressway carrying traffic from the Potomac bridges into the central city. These arrangements to improve arrival at destinations in the central city do not require high-speed traffic to be carried through the city at this point.

The new traffic pattern along E Street will free Pennsylvania Avenue for its ceremonial and symbolic functions and accelerate the distribution of central-city-bound travellers. The effect on Pennsylvania Avenue itself should mean more room for the tourists, government workers and shopping traffic, and fewer commercial vehicles, trucks and through traffic.

Parking will occupy two levels below the Ellipse and National Square. Additional parking at an underground level will be planned as part of the new buildings proposed for every site in the area between Pennsylvania Avenue and E Street and will also have direct access from the E Street roadway level. Detailed studies have been completed for the Ellipse area by Skidmore, Owings and Merrill, architects.

Eighth Street Axis

Midway between the Capitol and the White House, L'Enfant drew a grand cross-axis intended to relieve the diagonal of Pennsylvania Avenue and open a vista to the ridge on the north and to the Potomac river on the south. On the higher ground (where 8th Street now crosses F Street), L'Enfant proposed a national church for public ceremonies "and a proper shelter for monuments to those who fell in the cause of liberty." This pantheon was to overlook a square at Pennsylvania Avenue containing a "grand fountain intended with a constant spurt of water." A market was built at the south side of the fountain square at the lip of the Tiber Canal, which L'Enfant carried straight through the center of all the civic grandeur.

Thus, from the beginning, the commercial life and the national life of the capital were to be linked. The cross-axis at 8th Street was intended not only to add another dimension to the powerful geometry of L'Enfant's spatial composition but also to join these functions. In the Pennsylvania Avenue Commission's plan, both objectives of the capital's first planner, never more important than today, will be realized.

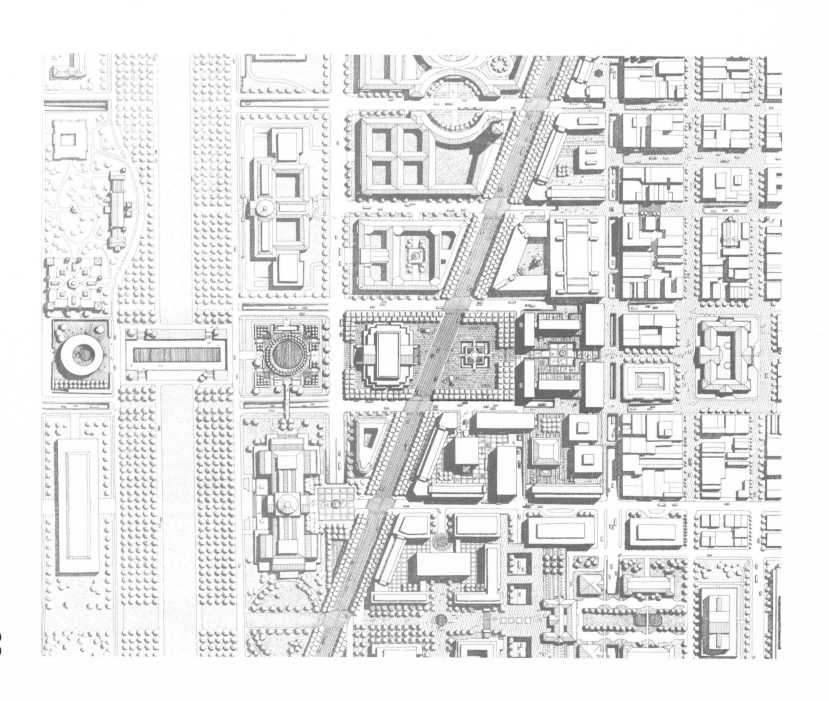

Opening at 8th Street, a pedestrian mall will cascade from F Street on the north, where the National Portrait Gallery projects into the busy retail center, to a great new Market Square on the Avenue. Continuing south of the Avenue the new minor-axis will cross Constitution Avenue beyond the Archives Building and merge with the National Gallery sculpture garden leading to the Joseph H. Hirshhorn Museum, on the south side of the mall.

The new 8th Street cross-axis offers an unexcelled opportunity to link the downtown retail core proposed by Downtown Progress and the complex of government buildings south of Pennsylvania Avenue. Visitors will find it easy to visit both in a single morning of sight-seeing and shopping.

Development of the 8th Street cross-axis, beginning with Market Square, will stimulate new private enterprise long sought for this central area by the businessmen of the National Capital Downtown Committee, Inc. Prestige hotels and private office buildings along the axis will benefit each other; an additional stimulus will come from the establishment of the International Center for Scholars authorized by Congress as a memorial to President Woodrow Wilson in the quadrangle north of Market Square. These new uses

Existing conditions along the 8th Street Axis.

29

will, in turn, attract theaters, movies and fine restaurants to enhance the value of the area as a major center of the metropolitan community.

The recent opening of the National Portrait Gallery and the National Collection of Fine Arts in the old Patent Office building on F Street shows how public initiative can stimulate private action. New art stores, bookshops and other high-value retailing have appeared across from the Gallery; store fronts have been smartened up; and other investors are studying the area.

The renovated Portrait Gallery occupies the site L'Enfant intended for a national church. Located athwart 8th Street and extending from 7th to 9th, this 1836 building defines the width allotted to the cross-axis. Today between this historic building and Pennsylvania Avenue stretches an area of unrestored 19th century buildings, many unoccupied above the first floor. This area separates the government buildings south of Pennsylvania Avenue from the commercial resources of the F Street Mall. The new cross-axis design will improve the flow between these areas. By closing 8th Street and rebuilding the blocks between 7th and 9th and the adjacent blocks between 7th and 6th, will be opened for a lively mixture of public and private development.

Model of the completed 8th Street Axis.

30

Market Square

The new urbanity will be fully expressed in Market Square, to be developed as a paved and landscaped plaza just north of Pennsylvania Avenue. Here, small shops, restaurants, and a permanent outdoor exhibition pavilion for the National Archives will invite public use and enjoyment. Nor will the new liveliness end at sundown, when the government buildings now become a deserted city; these resources will be open for night-time use, reinforcing the trend pioneered by the Smithsonian Institution, which recently opened its museums on the south side of Pennsylvania Avenue for use in evening hours. The Federal initiative in introducing a new level of urban delight to the Pennsylvania Avenue area will attract private development of a comparable standard.

Traffic on 7th and 9th Streets will be hidden beneath the deck north of the square and thus not lessen

The proposed site for the Market Square and Woodrow Wilson Memorial.

31

the pleasure of this attractive path between Pennsylvania Avenue and F Street. Two levels of parking provided under Market Square, parts of the cross-axis and the adjoining new buildings will free the entire area of the parked cars which now blot out the esthetic satisfactions contrived by two centuries of Federal planning and building. One-third of the land needed to develop the 8th Street cross-axis is already in public ownership: buildings, streets and small plots displaying monuments. The Commission recommends that the "public purpose" for which land condemnation has been authorized include additional land for private building in this cross-axis area, and that land so condemned by the government be sold to private investors at a written-down price that will make redevelopment possible. This unparalleled opportunity to regenerate the central city of Washington can be realized without substantial public funding; the Commission estimates that closed streets alone will double the land available for building.

Model of the completed Market Square and the Woodrow Wilson Center,

Woodrow Wilson Center

The life of urban design is in its expression of the purposes of a city—and in this case, of a nation. A national purpose not so far expressed in the capital design will be seen in the International Center for Scholars to be built as a living memorial to Woodrow Wilson on the 8th Street cross-axis north of Market Square.

The Woodrow Wilson Center will promote the study of government, international affairs, history and related disciplines by giving its scholars immediate access to the historic documents of the National Archives building, the Library of Congress, and the resources of the great museums of the Smithsonian Institution. The distinguished members of the Woodrow Wilson Memorial Commission established by Congress in 1961 hope that the Center's scholars will be able to study the living history being made at their elbow and to contribute understanding and analysis that will help to shape it.

In its final report, the Woodrow Wilson Memorial Commission recommended that the International Center for Scholars be built on the 8th Street site as shown on page 33. The Commission further recommended that

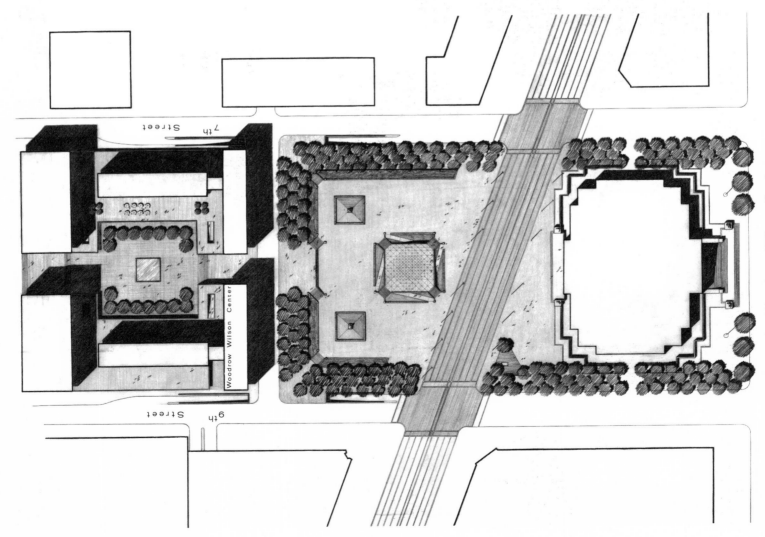

Plan of Market Square and the Woodrow Wilson Center.

33

a permanent endowment fund of $30,000,000, providing an annual operating income of $1,500,000, be sought from Federal appropriations and matching contributions by private philanthropic foundations in the United States and other countries. The Pennsylvania Avenue Commission has approved the site for the Memorial located adjacent to Market Square on the north. It also recommends that the site be given to the Center by the nation. Congress has approved the basic concept of the Woodrow Wilson Memorial in an act signed into law on October 24, 1968, by the President. This act created an 8-member board appointed by the President to prepare plans and specifications for the Center. The Board will be funded by a $200,000 appropriation for the 1970 fiscal year. Once the precise space requirements are determined, it will be possible to establish whether one or both buildings on the north of the Square are needed.

Like other elements of the Pennsylvania Avenue plan, the Center will be a place of lively activity. While it will provide residence and secluded offices and meeting rooms for its Fellows and scholarly visitors, it will also have public exhibition areas, seminar and dining facilities and an information center, indexing the scholarly resources of the Washington area. Scholars from the city's universities and many research

Artist's sketch looking south from the Woodrow Wilson Center.

34

institutions as well as staff members of Federal agencies will participate in Center activities.

On the south side of Pennsylvania Avenue, John Russell Pope's National Archives building, guardian of the Constitution and the Bill of Rights, stands on the site of the market in L'Enfant's original plan. This classic building squarely faces the National Portrait Gallery four blocks to the north, demonstrating L'Enfant's intended cross-axis.

National Gallery of Art Sculpture Garden

In the now vacant block immediately south of the National Archives, the National Gallery of Art will construct a sculpture garden and pool. The circular pool, enclosed by formal gardens, will be used for ice skating in season. The National Capital Planning Commission and the Fine Arts Commission have approved the design. Architects for this project are Skidmore, Owings and Merrill. The current estimate for construction of this outdoor exhibit facility is $3 million. The National Park Service will seek preliminary funding in this session of Congress.

Model of the proposed National Gallery of Art Sculpture Garden.

35

Hirshhorn Museum

The 8th Street cross-axis will continue across the Mall as a sunken sculpture court and reflecting pool between landscaped walkways leading to the Joseph H. Hirshhorn Museum. The Museum building will itself be lifted above the walkway on great concrete arches, leaving the pedestrian path uninterrupted. A marble-faced cylinder enclosing three levels of gallery space, the new Museum will stand between the brownstone turrets of the Smithsonian Institution's Arts and Industries Building and the projected Air and Space Museum.

The 60-foot-high building will house approximately 5600 works of art given by Joseph Hirshhorn to the people of the United States. The inner glass wall of the cylindrical building will give a continuous view of the inner court, 115 feet in diameter, as visitors move along the inner corridor which opens onto the galleries, all placed in the windowless part of the building. From the second gallery level, a wide balcony overlooks the axial vista northward across the Mall to the National Archives building.

Model of the Hirshhorn Museum and its sculpture garden crossing the Mall.

36

The building plan has been approved by the National Capital Planning Commission and by the Fine Arts Commission, whose members commended the architectural design. Congress appropriated $800,000 for planning the Museum and its sculpture garden in 1967 and has authorized building contract obligations totaling $50 million. Of this sum, $2 million has been appropriated, and construction will begin in the spring.

Artist's sketch of the Hirshhorn Museum.

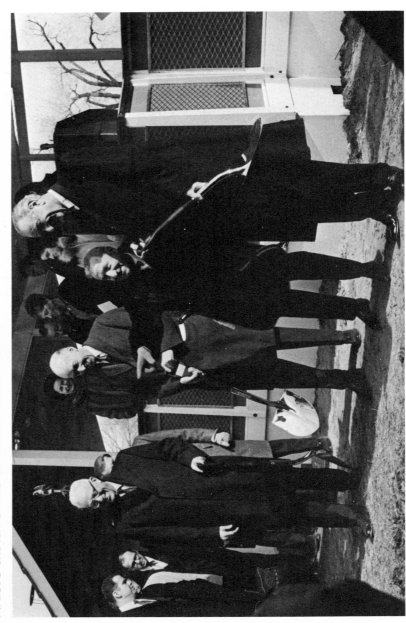

Ground-breaking ceremony for the Hirshhorn Museum, January 8, 1969.

F.B.I. Building

A pedestrian plaza extending across its entire block is part of a two-million-square-foot building now under construction along the north side of Pennsylvania Avenue for the Department of Justice. The building occupies the block between 9th and 10th Streets and faces the Department of Justice headquarters building on the south side of the Avenue. This massive and important structure is a key part of the Commission's proposal for public and private buildings to function together in the Pennsylvania Avenue area—a long-range plan to be realized by many builders over the decade ahead.

Set back 50 feet from the present building line, the structure conforms to the provision for a 76-foot-wide sidewalk along the ceremonial Avenue. The building height will be 107 feet at the front, a height respecting the 120-foot maximum height proposed for new buildings east of 10th Street on the north side of the Avenue. The building site, at the lowest point of Pennsylvania Avenue, slopes up 17 feet to E Street on its northern perimeter, where the building height will be 160 feet.

Some 7000 tourists daily now view the FBI's crime-fighting resources, and 10,000 are expected by 1970.

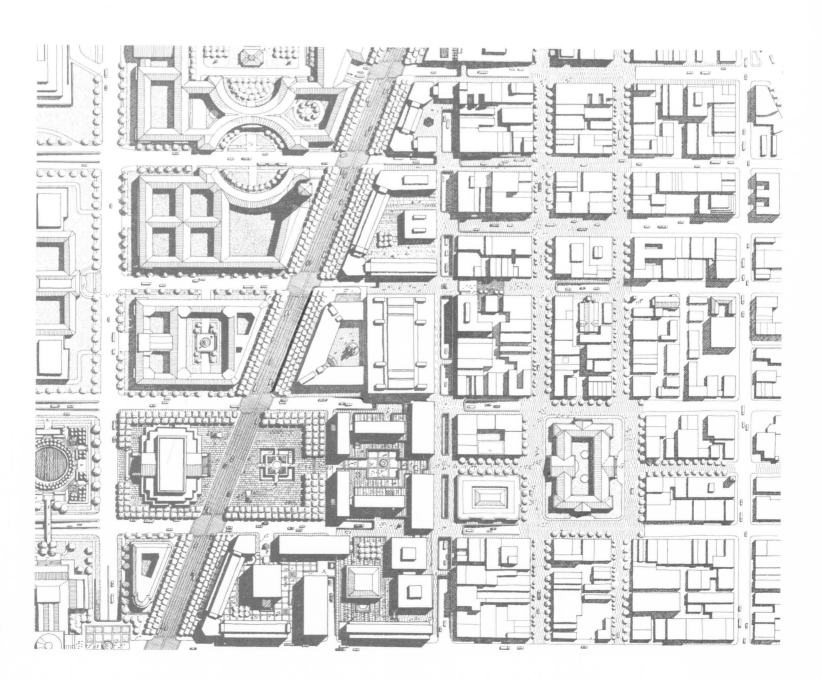

Visitors to the new FBI building will enter from E Street at ground level through a landscaped plaza that leads to an arcade overlooking Pennsylvania Avenue. On this side, the plaza will be at second floor level. While security reasons bar use of this plaza for the small shops and refreshment facilities planned to enliven other pedestrian areas along the Avenue, it will nevertheless be an open public pathway.

To ascend from the plaza, visitors have open access to escalators in two service cores 123 feet high. Six other service cores will house controlled-access elevators serving all floors. By this vertical articulation of traffic, the architects solved a major design problem—the need to open the building to visitors while protecting the agency's security.

Site of FBI Building, presently under construction.

39

Model of the completed FBI Building.

Three underground parking levels will be reached from E Street, which, at a future date, is to be a depressed roadway running along the northern boundary of the site. The increased height of the E Street side of the building is dramatized by lifting this section on columns above a glass-walled dining area that will adjoin a roof garden. The T-shape of the post-and-lintel construction is the basic design element of the building. Precast and poured-in-place concrete elements will have the soft sandy tones of Potomac gravel, given by aggregate graded from rock size. Chip size aggregate will be used for the major part of the building facade.

Congress appropriated $11 million for the first phase of construction to be completed by December 1969; this stage will comprise excavation, foundations, and the perimeter walls to the first basement level. The remainder of construction, for which Congress will be asked to appropriate $49 million, is scheduled for award in early 1971 and for completion by 1974.

Architect's rendering of the completed FBI Building.

41

Federal Triangle

The plan for the Federal Triangle, originally conceived in 1902 by the McMillan Park Commission, responds to one of the rare opportunities in city building to achieve a large-scale building complex of unified design. Significant original elements remained incomplete when the nation faced the depression of the 1930's. As part of the Pennsylvania Avenue Plan, these gaps will now be filled and the full Triangle concept be realized.

To this end, the Pennsylvania Avenue Commission recommends additions to two buildings and the improvement of both the Grand Plaza, potentially one of the finest urban spaces in the country, and the Great Circle on 12th Street. The Commission's plan calls for removing 13th Street south of its intersection with E Street (page 45); its pathway south of Pennsylvania Avenue will become part of the Grand Plaza. With underground parking to rescue its surface for landscaping, the Plaza will be designed as a formal garden-park extending from the Commerce building's 14th Street facade to the half-circle formed by the original Post Office Department building.

The Pennsylvania Avenue Commission has endorsed

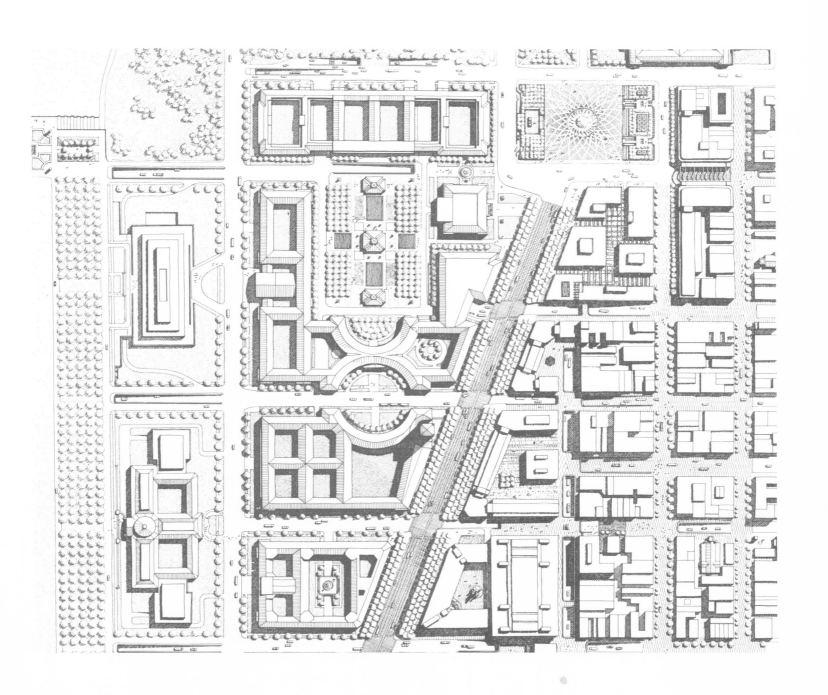

the plan for the Triangle shown in the model (page 44) and the following diagram (page 45). Architect John Carl Warnecke, jr. proposes that the design of the addition to the Post Office Department should link the classic style of the Federal Triangle to the contemporary architectural forms of the buildings already rising on the north side of the Avenue. The cavernous old Post Office building will be torn down, and its 360-foot-high clock tower, a cherished landmark, will be restored as a tourist orientation center to enliven Pennsylvania Avenue.

The extension of the Post Office Department building will provide some 500-600,000 square feet at a cost estimated at $20-24 million. Completing the Great Circle will give the Internal Revenue Service 350,000 square feet at a cost estimated at $20 million.

The existing Federal Triangle, and the congested parking in the Grand Plaza.

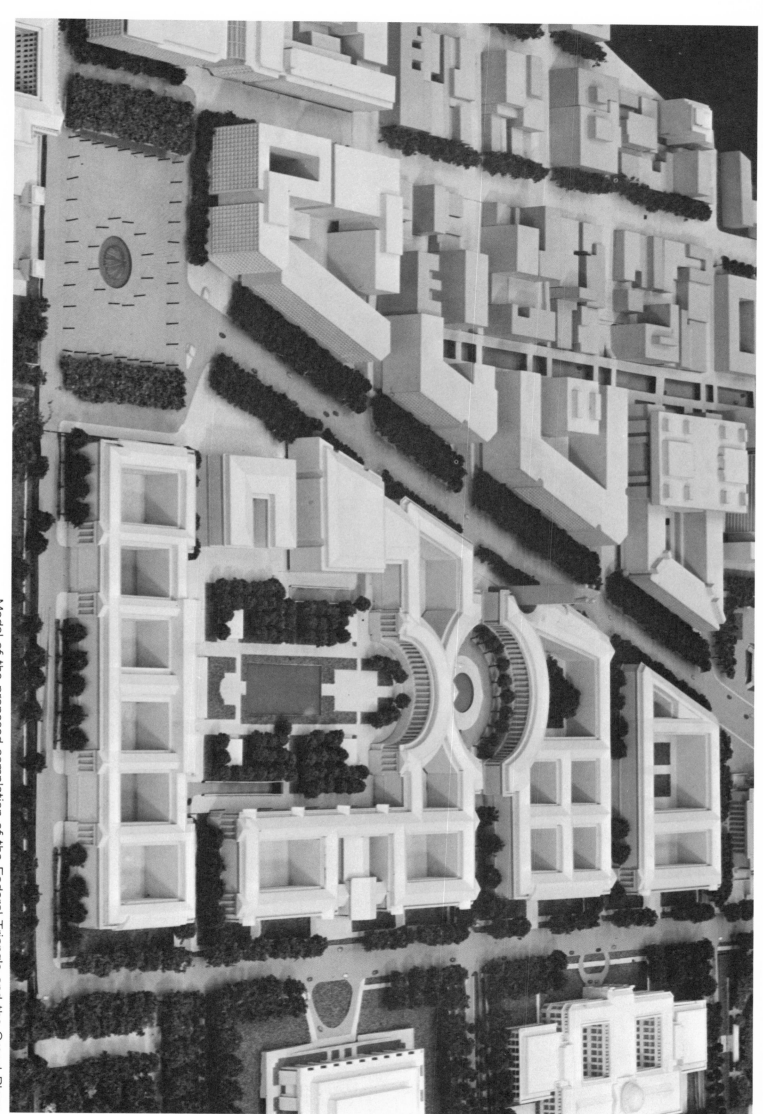

Model of the proposed completion of the Federal Triangle and the Grand Plaza.

44

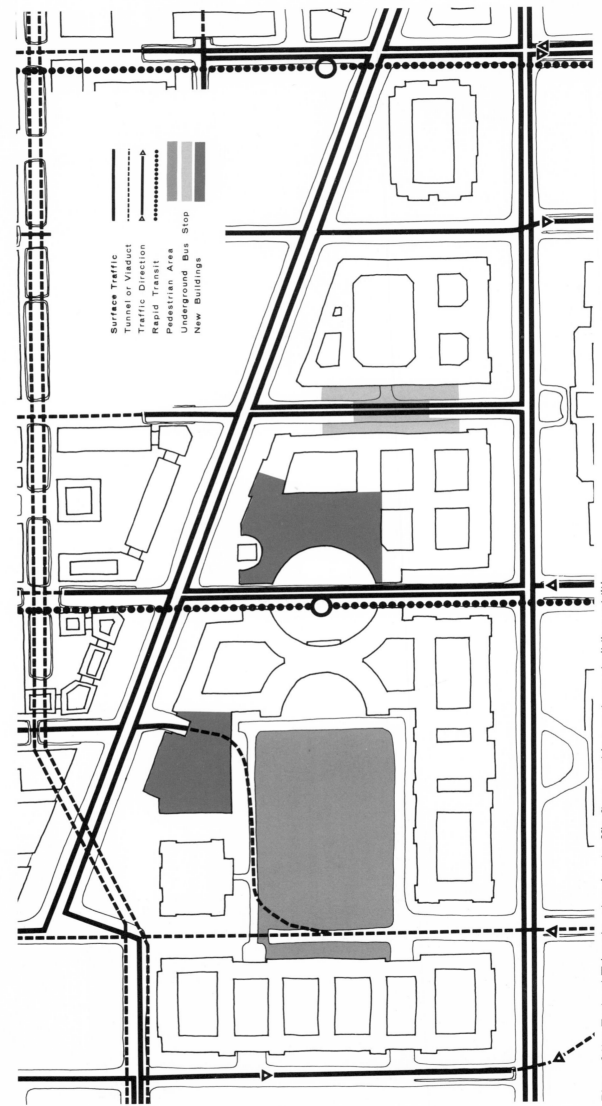

Surface Traffic
Tunnel or Viaduct
Traffic Direction
Rapid Transit
Pedestrian Area
Underground Bus Stop
New Buildings

Plan of the Federal Triangle, showing traffic flow, parking and new building additions.

45

Many of the 24,000 government employees who work in the Federal Triangle drive to work and park in the Great Circle and the Grand Plaza. Others use the suburban buses that now crowd Pennsylvania Avenue in front of the old Post Office building or city buses that line 13th Street. These improvisations are inconvenient, inefficient and unsightly. The new plan will park 1600 cars underneath the Plaza. A new underground bus terminal will rechannel buses below 10th Street between the Justice Department and Internal Revenue buildings. The rapid transit system expected by 1972 will also have a station below the Great Circle at 12th Street. Thus the below-ground level will become a major transfer point for workers using public transportation.

Free from automobiles and buses, the Grand Plaza will become what it was originally intended to be: a calm, dignified, formal space at the center of the city. Set among trees and other green landscaping, a central reflecting pool will add its cool sparkle.

The sea of cars presently in the Grand Plaza.

46

A two-story gallery in the Internal Revenue Service building, flanked by services for visitors, will lead from a richly landscaped interior courtyard to the Great Circle. Trees will be omitted to heighten the effectiveness of the circular building facades, and the area around the central fountain will be paved.

Because the Internal Revenue Service addition will complete the Great Circle started by the classic Post Office building, the architects recommend repeating the classic style here. For the less dependent Post Office Department addition, they recommend the inventive neo-classic re-interpretation shown here, replacing the Doric order with simple columnar shapes suited to modern building materials and technology. The projecting porticos are retained but much simplified and without pediments. The great cornice is notable as a translation to modern idiom; it permits windows not in the older building while shading the wide glass areas. The third floor terrace and the arcade match similar elements planned for buildings on the north side of the Avenue.

The National Capital Planning Commission has given preliminary approval to plans for both building additions for budgetary purposes and will further review the plans at a more advanced stage.

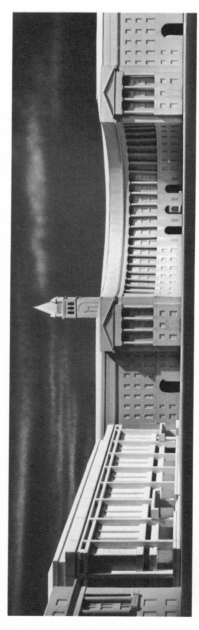

Model of the completed Grand Plaza.

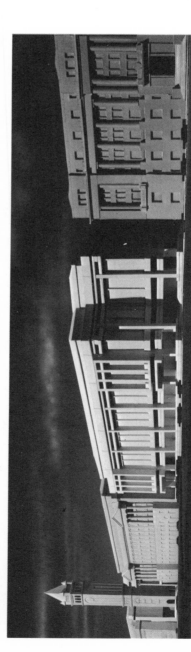

Model of the new Post Office Building as seen from Pennsylvania Avenue.

47

Presidential Building

What happens when decaying downtown blocks are opened to light and air can be seen in the 12-story buff concrete and bronze glass Presidential Building. Completed in July, 1968 at Pennsylvania Avenue and 12th Street, it is the first private development to meet the rebuilding standards outlined by the President's Advisory Council.

Collaboration between government and private enterprise made this handsome building possible. The developer, the building owners, and the District Government, the Fine Arts Commission, and the National Capital Planning Commission have made the Presidential Building a prototype of what the Avenue will be. It shows how private builders can conform to a large-scale plan to gain an improved architectural environment.

The Presidential Building is also the first in a series of many buildings to utilize the sectional development plans under Article 75 of the Zoning Regulations of the District of Columbia. Sectional development provides additional advantages to the developer by providing the benefits of large-scale development to the small entrepreneur building a single structure. The Zoning Commission,

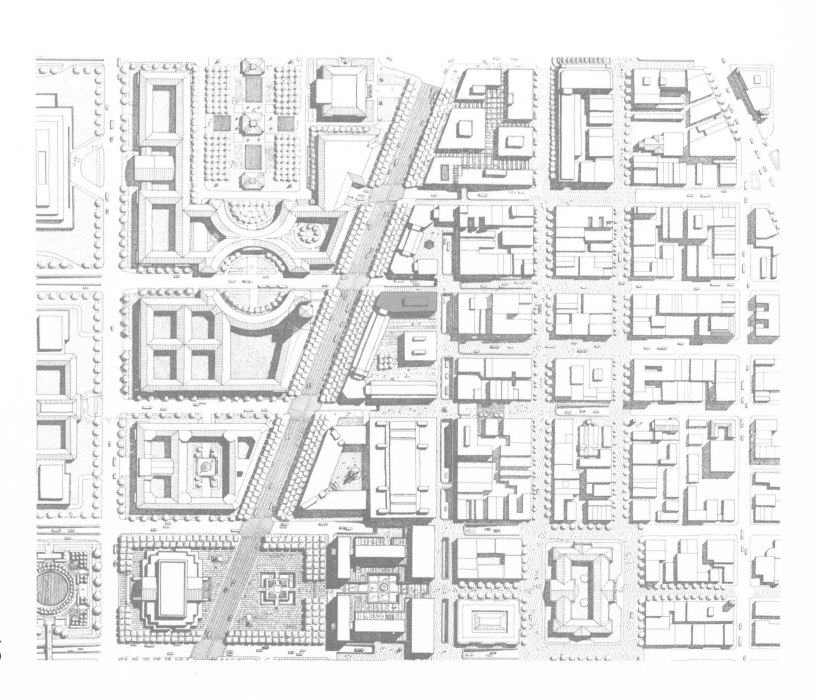

Fine Arts Commission, and the District government worked closely with the Pennsylvania Avenue Commission to implement the plans and have expressed their desire to have other blocks along the Avenue developed in the same manner.

The owners set their building back 50 feet from the present building line (which on Pennsylvania Avenue is already 26 feet back from the curb) to provide the broad sidewalk planned for the entire north side of Pennsylvania Avenue between the White House and the Capitol. The resulting 76-foot-wide pedestrian walkway, paved in brick and landscaped, will serve as a grandstand along Washington's chief ceremonial avenue.

The third-floor level of the new building overlooks the 76-foot-wide Avenue sidewalk and a railed balcony

The Presidential Building and the pilot landscaping project for the Avenue.

49

on the second floor. The balcony extends the "grand-stand" provided by the wide sidewalk; it will offer preferred seats for ceremonial events along the Avenue. On 12th Street, the third floor of the building is cantilevered 14 feet out from massive concrete columns, cast on the site. The overhang forms an arcade, sheltering the walker from rain and sun.

A wing of the building extending across the back of the site to 11th Street was kept low to allow for later completion of the open square at the center of the block. This interior square will be part of the automobile-free pedestrian shelf to extend from F Street to Pennsylvania Avenue, where it will be one floor above the present street level (page 27). The rear wing provides access to four levels of underground parking along E Street, which will become a depressed roadway.

Model of the Presidential Building with the completed block development.

50

The pilot landscaping project of the Avenue in front of the Presidential Building shows how landscape architect Dan Kiley intends to enrich the Avenue with linden trees and plants in three dense sculptured rows. Each curb tier is finished in rose Minnesota granite, which also rims the raised planter boxes, broad enough to yield seating space. The 76-foot-wide sidewalk also acts as a plaza for the main building entrance and makes us realize how effectively such a forecourt can display a city building.

The model landscaping for the Presidential Building was dedicated on November 18, 1968. Honored guests were Mrs. Lyndon Johnson, Secretary of the Interior Stewart L. Udall, and Deputy Commissioner Thomas Fletcher.

Nathaniel Owings and Mrs. Lyndon B. Johnson. Pilot landscaping project, November 1968.

Finish work being done before the dedication.

Workmen installing the paved surface.

51

Superblock

The superblock is the module of a new kind of city. Rebuilding to superblock design, as planned for the block between 13th and 14th, will set tall buildings in a network of open spaces that will be at once a joy to the users and a magic multiplier of that real estate premium: front footage. Valuable front footage is added by a plaza inside the block, landscaped and edged by shops, restaurants and other attractions. By planning together rather than separately, building investors salvage central space that will benefit them all.

In its work with municipal authorities and private investors, the Commission has sought to bring about an interplay of motives and ideas to realize a building initiative that is more than the sum of individual decisions. Only private resources can bring about the liveliness and variety that give urbanity its meaning: the city as meeting place and market place, where ideas are exchanged as well as goods.

The Commission has tried to find what can best be done in common — as, for example, providing underground parking with all buildings sharing ramp access (one way of saving space) or joint utilities (one way of

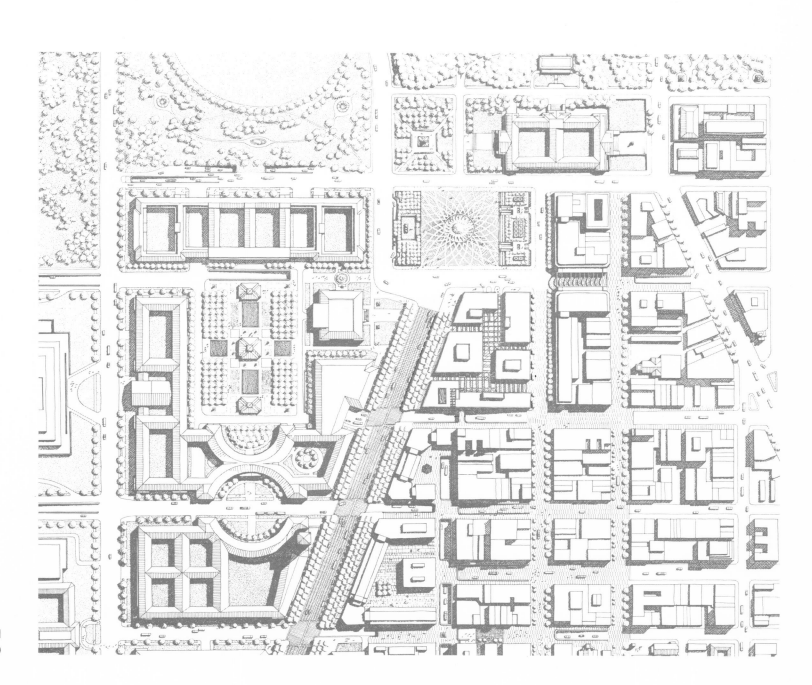

cutting operating costs) with the central heating plant designed to eliminate a major source of air pollution—and what can best be done separately. Such a rational assignment of responsibilities is remote from the urban anarchy of the past.

Superblock design principles will also guide architectural solutions for the new blocks north of Pennsylvania Avenue. The Commission's economic and real estate consultants have shown that the proposed new buildings will yield from $500 to $600 million in new private investment and increase the city's tax revenue by an estimated 20 per cent. Along the north side of the Avenue, in a 40-acre area betwen 6th and 14th Streets, some 5.2 million square feet of new private building is contemplated, mixed with government and institutional uses amounting to 6.1 million square feet.

Some of the country's leading land developers and

The proposed site for the Superblock.

53

building entrepreneurs are working closely with the Commission. Out of this work have come a number of specific proposals for rebuilding. In this particular block, studies have been made for two hotels: one a convention-type hotel equipped for large meetings, the other a luxury hotel overlooking National Square and suitable for Washington's many prominent international visitors.

In the phase diagrams (page 54), it will be noted that the first superblock building unit extends over E Street as an "air rights" development.

A continuing elevated pedestrian platform, extending from F Street above the depressed pathway of E Street and descending by stages to the level of Pennsylvania Avenue, will unify the gardened superblock. The illustration (page 55) shows the central square as part of this uninterrupted platform.

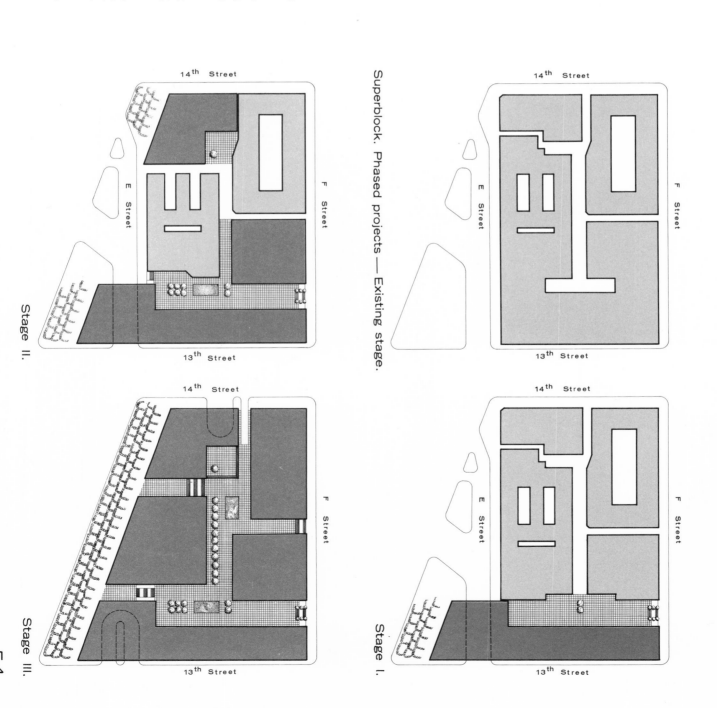

Superblock. Phased projects—Existing stage.

Stage I.

Stage II.

Stage III.

54

This plan multiplies the prized front footage by disposing shops and restaurants on three levels: the new level of the pedestrian deck, a balcony level, and the present street level. Three kinds of restaurants are planned: low-priced cafeterias at the ground level, a moderate-priced restaurant with an outdoor cafe at the pedestrian deck, and a luxury restaurant with a city-wide view at rooftop. This and many other kinds of multi-use developments are planned so that this central city will not die every night when the big offices turn out their lights.

Daniel Patrick Moynihan, the Commission's vice-chairman, has said: "It is open to us in this time and in this place to build the first modern central city in the world."

Artist's sketch of the interior glass-covered air-conditioned shopping arcade.

55

National Square

Grand vista for Pennsylvania Avenue and entry court of the White House, National Square will extend between the Commerce Building on the south to F Street on the north. At the Square's western edge, a monumental gate leading to the White House grounds has been proposed by the Commission to symbolize and serve as a reception area for White House visitors who arrive at an average rate of 6000 a day.

Under the Square, parking space will accommodate 600 cars, with direct entry from the E Street tunnel and the perimeter surface streets. Thus a visitor entering Washington along the south leg of the new inner freeway can proceed directly to downtown Washington via the E Street tunnel and reach the parking area under National Square or the adjacent Ellipse.

By escalator, the visitor will ascend to the Square. Here he will be able to have lunch atop the wide belvedere to be raised along the north side of the Square or visit the stores, restaurants and cinemas below. Or he can move along a glass-covered galleria of shops in line with the present path of 14th Street north of F Street.

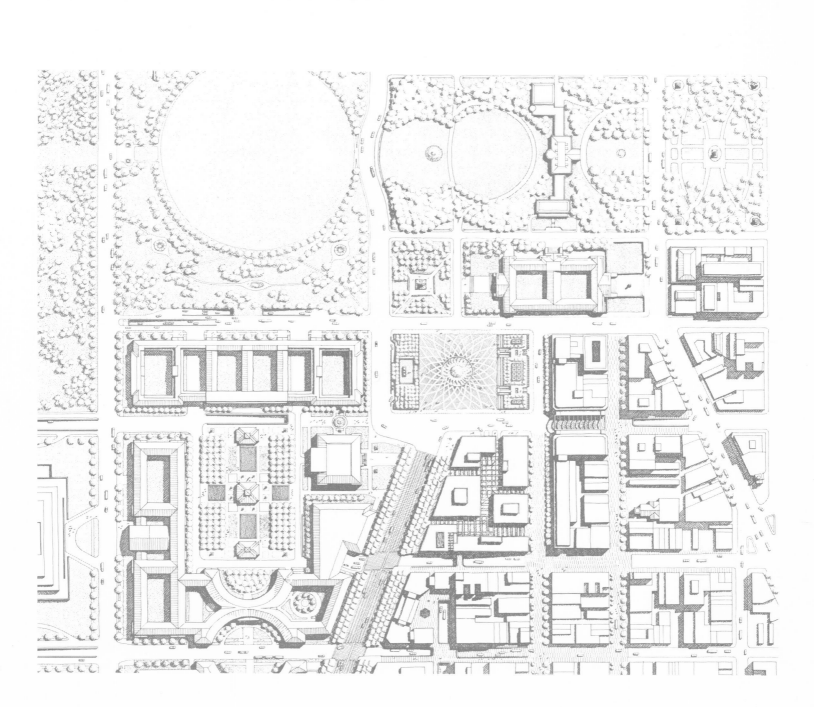

National Square will occupy the block between 14th and 15th Streets. While the 1964 Avenue report proposed also to include half the block between 13th and 14th Streets, continued study has led the Commission to recommend that 14th Street be the Square's eastern boundary. Both the National Capital Planning Commission and the Fine Arts Commission have approved this plan for the square in principle.

Under authority granted by the National Historic Sites Act of 1935, Secretary of the Interior Stewart Udall in October, 1968 asked the General Services Administration to negotiate an exchange of federal surplus land for the Willard Hotel, which closed July, 1968. Negotiations for the trade of the Willard Hotel and the acquisition of adjacent properties are still in progress.

The site, as it now exists, for National Square.

Model of National Square, looking north to the Belvedere.

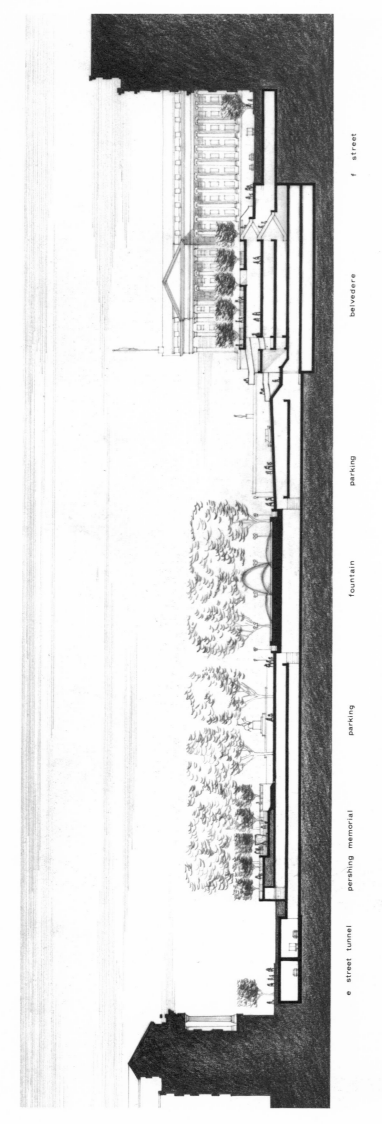

e street tunnel   pershing memorial   parking   fountain   parking   belvedere   f street

Vertical north-south section through National Square.

A memorial to General John Pershing, authorized by Congress in 1967, will occupy the tiered and landscaped strip to the south, bounded by 14th and 15th Streets. The Commission proposes that the 150 foot diameter fountain, designated for the center of the Square become a focal element in the design of the Pershing Memorial and the Avenue. The American Battle Monuments Commission will seek definitive design funds in this session of Congress.

The dynamic potential of the Pennylvania Avenue Plan rests in the development of National Square. In its original Report to the President, the Pennsylvania Avenue Council promised an avenue which would be "lively, friendly and inviting, as well as dignified and impressive." As the principal locus for tourist and commercial activity, National Square will generate the color and diversity, dignity and impressiveness required for the success of the total plan.

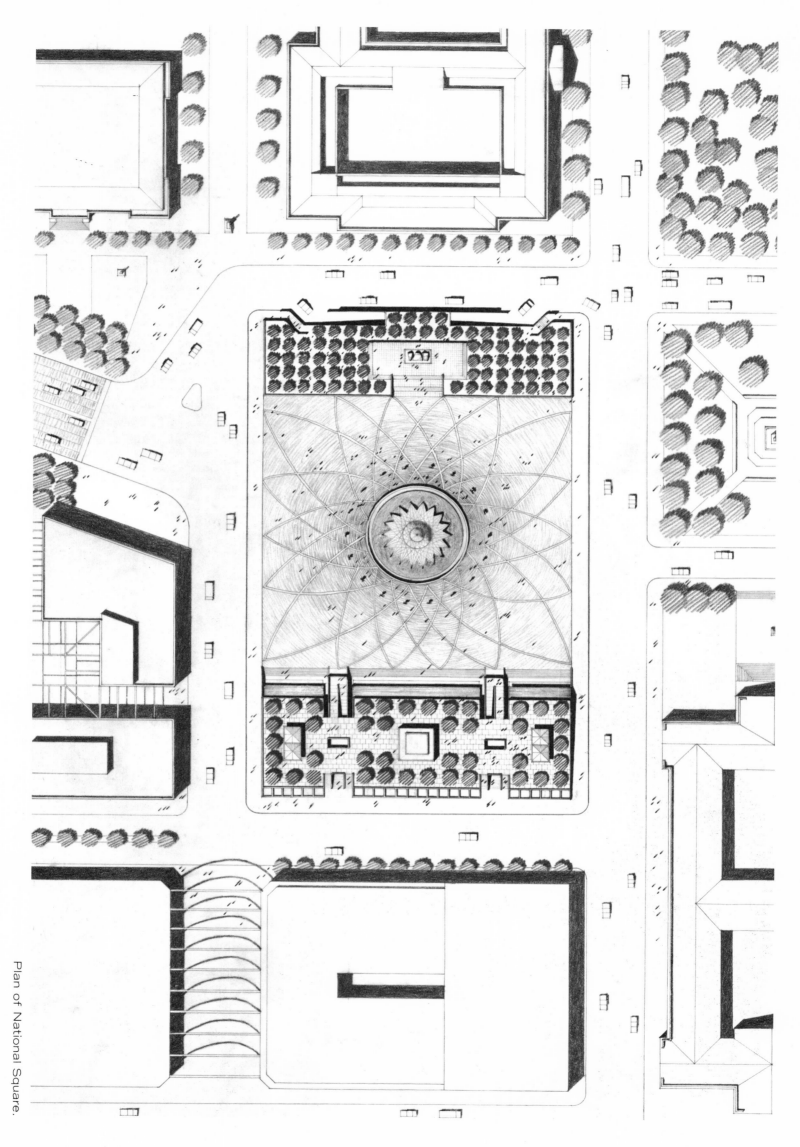

The Avenue and the Future

This review of planning and development along the entire length of Pennsylvania Avenue must certainly yield two conclusions. The first is that the Avenue is more than the sum of its separate developmental activities. Important as they are, they are but steps to realizing the plan for the Avenue as a whole. The second is that while everything that is taking place conforms to the original concepts of the Council plan of 1964, extensive design changes have been made in that document. Without the Pennsylvania Avenue Commission to keep alive the original goals and basic outlines of the plan, and to reinterpret and apply its recommendations to the constantly changing demands of government and private developers, the progress achieved to date would have been impossible. Without this steady and sustained special interest, the separate developments would go their own individual ways, and not contribute to the larger objectives of the development of the

Model of the proposed Pennsylvania Avenue looking from the White House to the Capitol.

61

Avenue as a whole. An effort to apply mechanically and in detail the concept plan originally proposed would certainly have led nowhere.

As a living document and a continuing process, the Pennsylvania Avenue plan has responded creatively to new demands and opportunities. The increased sophistication with which the demands of circulation, traffic and parking have been met exhibits a collaboration between the Commission, its design staff and its specialized consultants, working with local and Federal agencies and private developers. Such capability cannot be developed overnight or to order. The still-evolving concept of the superblock is another illustration of the Commission's creative ability. Here a new concept, not found in the original plan for the Avenue but entirely compatible with it in letter and spirit, has been developed in recognition of demands by private business for sites in this area. Essential to the unified design of the Avenue from the Capitol to the White House are the uniform setback and height limits for buildings. The commodious sidewalk space provided for pedestrians is reinforced by a system of continuous arcades above the walks. Special paving and plantings, unique street signs and lighting further enhance the basic architectural and circulatory improvements provided by the plan.

The Pennsylvania Avenue Commission's continuing attention is essential if the rapid pace of the Avenue's development is to continue. The momentum gained in the past years must not be lost. If the work of the Commission is to go forward and its goals be realized, a new scale of design refinement must be reached. To accomplish this, it is proposed that the following specific recommendations be implemented:

1. Clearly establish the Pennsylvania Avenue Commission with authority to insure that the recommendations and principles set down by the Council and by the Commission are incorporated in specific detail by private or public developers and agencies.

2. Obtain funds to prepare Sectional Development plans for each block on the north side of Pennsylvania Avenue between 15th and 6th Streets.

3. Conduct a detailed study of the proposed E Street distributor system, linking it with the proposed street plans for the District.

4. Prepare detail designs for the public spaces designated in the Plan and obtain acquisition authority and funds to develop them.

5. Establish a public parking authority to insure the development of needed parking facilities in the downtown area.

6. Conduct, with the Smithsonian Institution, a feasibility study of the proposed Woodrow Wilson Memorial site. This would include the development of related private functions necessary to the Center's successful operation.

Set in the context of the future of the District of Columbia and its metropolitan area, Pennsylvania Avenue responds strongly to the dimensions of spectacular urban growth. By inviting metropolitan growth to channel itself into such new development opportunities, the plan avoids the waste of formless, anarchical and dispersed development. By adding a strong and coherent center, Washington gains rare civic identity that contributes to its municipal strength. Equally, it contributes to the strength of the Federal government whose functions will provide here, as in so many places throughout this capital city, the primary reason for the city's being. Not just practically, by providing sites for Federal buildings, an inviting and convenient working environment for hundreds of thousands of Federal workers, facilities for private employment, a larger tax base, and space and attractions for millions of visitors to the city annually; not just by ordering the use of urban space and the patterns of circulation; but by lifting up the hearts of all citizens and stimulating their pride, patriotism and strong sense of identification with their common heritage, the Pennsylvania Avenue plan builds on its historic past a new image of America's urban future.

Appendix a.

Executive Order

EXECUTIVE ORDER

ESTABLISHING A TEMPORARY COMMISSION ON PENNSYLVANIA AVENUE

WHEREAS Pennsylvania Avenue between the Capitol and the White House serves as the main ceremonial avenue connecting the centers of the Legislative and Executive Branches of the United States Government; and

WHEREAS parts of Pennsylvania Avenue have been in large measure developed in a manner consistent therewith; and

WHEREAS other parts of Pennsylvania Avenue have deteriorated in condition and design or are otherwise ill suited to the ceremonial purposes of the Avenue and to the National dignity; and

WHEREAS the President's Ad Hoc Committee on Federal Office Space called the attention of the President to the deterioration and obsolescence of Pennsylvania Avenue and recommended that he enlist the aid of the finest architectural talent in the Nation to develop plans for the improvement of Pennsylvania Avenue to reflect its National significance; and

WHEREAS the President requested distinguished members of the architectural and city planning profession to serve on a Council on Pennsylvania Avenue and to develop a plan for the improvement of the Avenue to a level commensurate with its National purpose; and

---

2

WHEREAS Congress, in support of this objective, appropriated funds to assist in the preparation of such plans; and

WHEREAS the President's Council on Pennsylvania Avenue has developed a general plan for the improvement of the Avenue, and the Council has been dissolved; and

WHEREAS the plan developed by the President's Council on Pennsylvania Avenue has been subjected to extensive review by the National Capital Planning Commission and other interested departments and agencies and has been deemed appropriate in its main outlines; and

WHEREAS the Congress will be asked to consider legislation to provide for the improvement of Pennsylvania Avenue:

NOW, THEREFORE, by virtue of the authority vested in me as President of the United States, it is hereby ordered as follows:

Section 1. Temporary Commission on Pennsylvania Avenue

(a) There is hereby established the Temporary Commission on Pennsylvania Avenue (hereinafter referred to as the Commission).

(b) The Commission shall be composed of the Secretary of the Interior, the Secretary of the Treasury, the Secretary of Labor, the Secretary of Commerce, the Attorney General, the Postmaster General, the Administrator of General Services, the Housing and Home Finance Administrator, the Chairman of the Commission of Fine Arts, the Chairman of the National Capital Planning Commission, the Secretary

---

3

of the Smithsonian Institution, the President of the Board of Commissioners of the District of Columbia, the Director of the National Gallery of Art, and such other members as may be appointed by the President. The Chairman shall invite the Architect of the Capitol to be a member of the Commission.

(c) The President shall appoint from among its members a Chairman of the Commission who shall direct its activities.

(d) Members of the Commission who are officers or employees of the Federal Government shall receive no additional compensation by virtue of membership on the Commission. Other members of the Commission shall be entitled to receive compensation and travel expenses, including per diem in lieu of subsistence, as authorized by law (5 U.S.C. 55a; 5 U.S.C. 73b-2) for persons in the Government service employed intermittently.

(e) The Commission shall meet at the call of the Chairman.

Sec. 2. Functions of the Commission

(a) The Commission shall advise the President with respect to the:

(1) the component parts of the general plan submitted by the President's Advisory Council on Pennsylvania Avenue respecting their feasibility and practicability from the standpoint of financial, engineering, planning, and other relevant considerations;

(2) the development of an orderly, phased program for carrying out the improvement of Pennsylvania Avenue;

4

(3) effects of the proposed improvements on owners and occupants of private property in and adjoining the area to be improved and actions respecting the improvement program that will assure its achievement with minimum harmful effects upon such private interests and with the least disruption of business within and adjoining the area;

(4) appropriate legislation for carrying out the program of improvement;

(b) Take steps to assure that such recommendations as it may develop respecting plans and programs for the improvement of Pennsylvania Avenue and the Comprehensive Plan for the National Capital and other plans prepared or being prepared by the National Capital Planning Commission are properly coordinated.

(c) Promote an understanding of the plan and its objectives among the public generally; and

(d) Undertake such other actions as may be permitted by law and requested by the President in furtherance of the objectives of this order.

Sec. 3. Commission staff and consultants

(a) The Chairman is authorized to appoint such personnel as may be necessary to assist the Commission in connection with the performance of its functions.

(b) The Commission is authorized to obtain services in accordance with the provisions of Section 15 of the Act of August 2, 1946 (5 U.S.C. 55a).

5

Sec. 4. Federal agencies

(a) As deemed necessary to facilitate the work of the Commission, the Chairman may request the head of any Executive department or agency whose activities may relate to the objectives of the Commission to designate a liaison officer to consult with the Commission on matters of common concern.

(b) Upon request of the Chairman, each Executive department or agency is authorized and directed, consistent with law, to furnish the Commission available information which the Commission may require in the performance of its functions.

(c) Each Federal agency represented on the Commission shall furnish such necessary assistance to the Commission as may be authorized by Section 214 of the Act of May 3, 1945, 59 Stat. 134 (31 U.S.C. 691).

(d) The National Capital Planning Commission is hereby designated as the agency which shall provide administrative services for the Commission.

THE WHITE HOUSE,

March 25, 1965

THE PENNSYLVANIA AVENUE NATIONAL HISTORIC SITE
WASHINGTON, D. C.

ORDER OF DESIGNATION

Secs. 461 et seq.) Declares it to be a national policy to preserve for public use historic sites, buildings, and objects of national significance for the inspiration and benefit of the people of the United States; and

WHEREAS, the act of August 21, 1935 (49 Stat. 666; 16 U.S.C.

WHEREAS, I have determined that certain lands in the city of Washington, District of Columbia, possess exceptional value in commemorating or illustrating the history of the United States within the meaning of the act of August 21, 1935, since within the area are situate Pennsylvania Avenue and historically related environs and since the area are said area possess national historical significance in the following manner:

...

NOW, THEREFORE, with the concurrence of Lyndon B. Johnson, President of the United States, I, Stewart L. Udall, Secretary of the Interior, by virtue of and pursuant to the authority vested in me under the act of Congress approved August 21, 1935, do hereby designate the following described lands to be a National Historic Site having the name "The Pennsylvania Avenue National Historic Site":

...

I CONCUR:

[signature]
PRESIDENT OF THE UNITED STATES

September 30, 1965

IN WITNESS WHEREOF, I have hereunto set my hand and caused the official seal of the Department of the Interior to be affixed in the city of Washington, District of Columbia, this thirtieth day of September 1965.

[signature]
Secretary of the Interior

Appendix C.

Woodrow Wilson Memorial Act

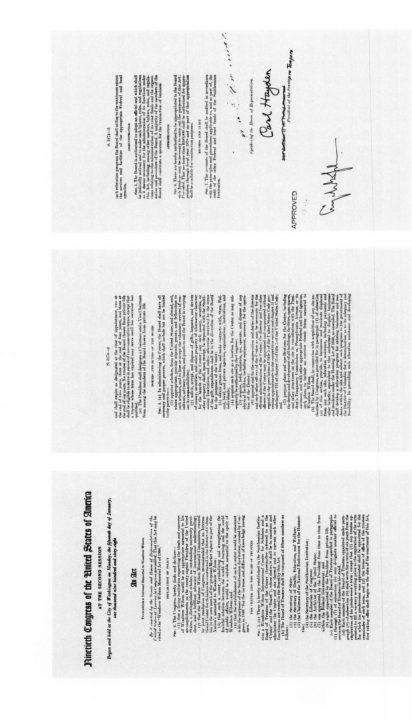

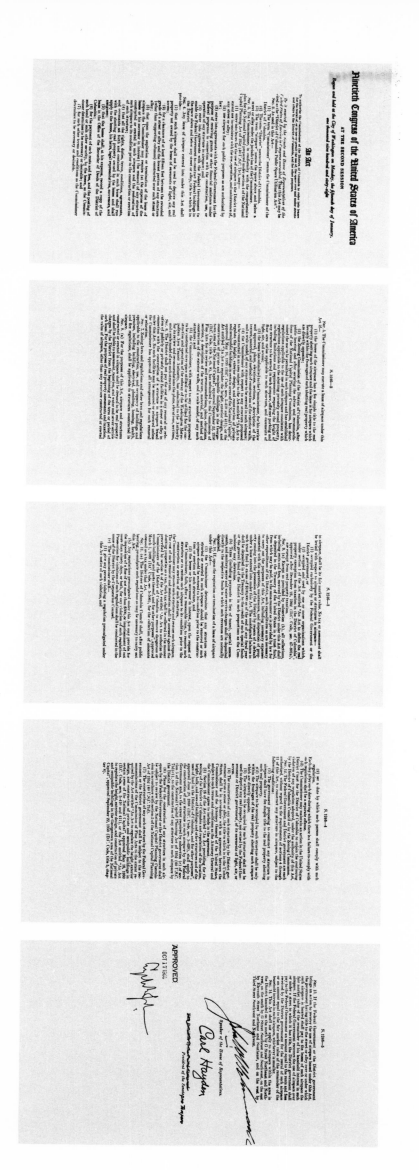

Acknowledgements

The progress described in this report was only possible through the work and advice of many individuals and organizations, both public and private, far too numerous to be listed here. Their willingness to donate time and energy demonstrated a widespread support for the plan, and the Commission gratefully acknowledges their invaluable aid.

Detail planning and design of this report was executed by David M. Childs, Catherine Henry, Eleanor M. McPeck and A. Herbert Ressing. John Galston, Lynn Dorsey and Fay Lebowitz contributed additional assistance. Frederick Gutheim, Special Consultant to the Commission, provided editorial supervision and overall guidance. Linda Mattison assisted Mr. Gutheim in editing the final version of the report. Louise Campbell prepared the initial draft.

Graphic Credits

Brooks, Barr, Graeber & White; Pitts, Mebane, Phelps & White: 17
Henry Beville: 20, 30, 32, 40, 44
Louis Checkman: 47
David Childs: 11, 16, 46, 50, 51, 59, 60
Dwain Faubion: 3, 10, 35, 58, 61
Al Harrell: 37
Helmut Jacoby: 41
Arthur Moore: 55
William Rohe: 23, 25, 26, 27, 45, 54
Skidmore, Owings & Merrill: 12, 37
Nicholas Solovioff: 13, 21, 22, 34
Ezra Stoller: 36
U. S. Air Force: 5, 24
Washington Evening Star: 51

69